PIANO | VOCAL | GUITAR

TIMELESS
CHRISTIAN SONGS
24 CCM & GOSPEL FAVORITES

ISBN 978-1-4950-0095-9

HAL•LEONARD® CORPORATION
7777 W. BLUEMOUND RD. P.O. BOX 13819 MILWAUKEE, WI 53213

Visit Hal Leonard Online at
www.halleonard.com

AWESOME GOD

Words and Music by
RICH MULLINS

BECAUSE HE LIVES

Words and Music by WILLIAM J. GAITHER
and GLORIA GAITHER

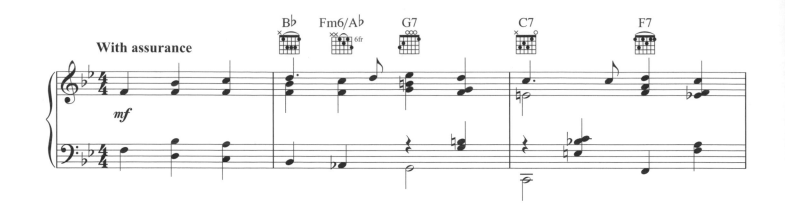

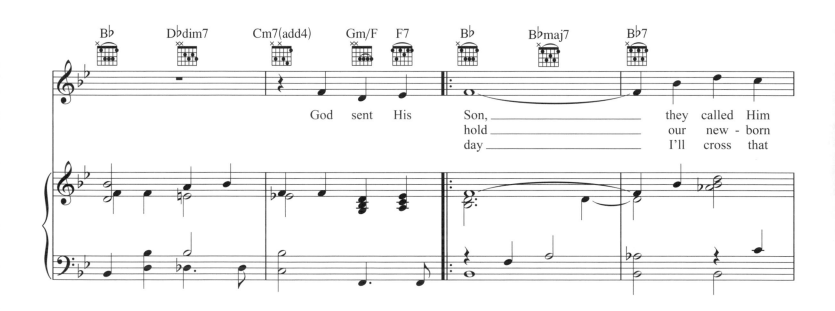

God sent His Son, _____ they called Him
hold _____ our new - born
day _____ I'll cross that

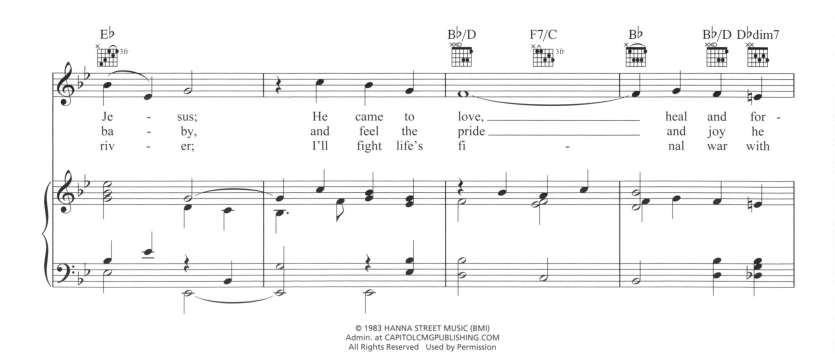

Je - sus; He came to love, _____ heal and for -
ba - by, and came to feel the pride _____ and joy he
riv - er; I'll fight life's fi - nal war with

AMAZING GRACE
(My Chains Are Gone)

Words by JOHN NEWTON
Traditional American Melody
Additional Words and Music by CHRIS TOMLIN
and LOUIE GIGLIO

EL SHADDAI

Words and Music by MICHAEL CARD
and JOHN THOMPSON

El Shad - dai, _____ El Shad - dai, _____ El El - yon _____ na A - do - nai, _____ age to age _____ You're still _____ the same, _____

FIND US FAITHFUL

Words and Music by
JON MOHR

FRIENDS

Words and Music by MICHAEL W. SMITH
and DEBORAH D. SMITH

keep the love _ that keeps _ us strong. And _

friends are friends _ for - ev - er if the Lord's the Lord _ of them. _ And a

friend will not _ say "nev - er," 'cause the wel - come will _ not end. _ Though it's

hard to let _ you go, _ in the Fa - ther's hands _ we know _ that a

GREAT IS THE LORD

Words and Music by MICHAEL W. SMITH
and DEBORAH D. SMITH

GLORIOUS DAY
(Living He Loved Me)

Words and Music by MARK HALL
and MICHAEL BLEAKER

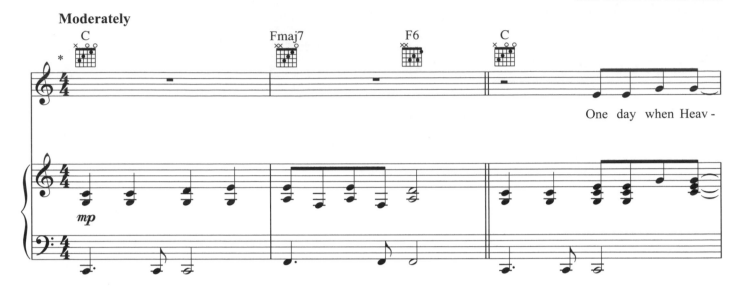

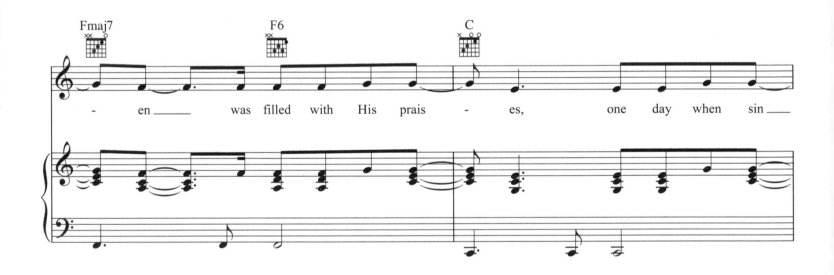

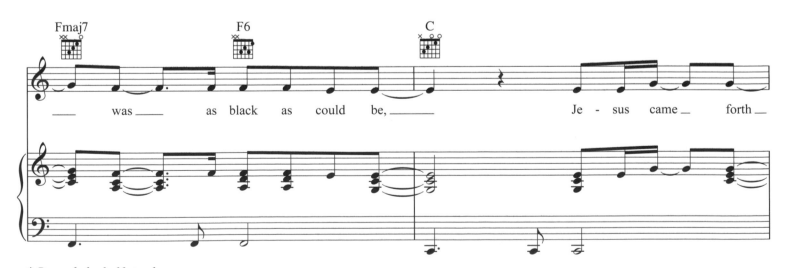

* Recorded a half step lower.

GOD WILL MAKE A WAY

Words and Music by
DON MOEN

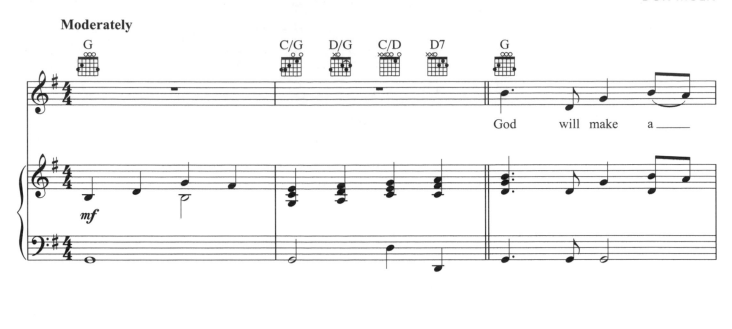

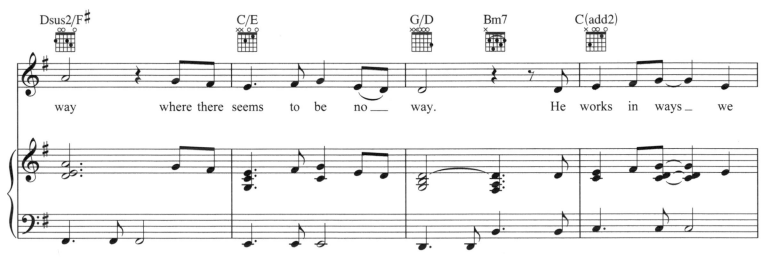

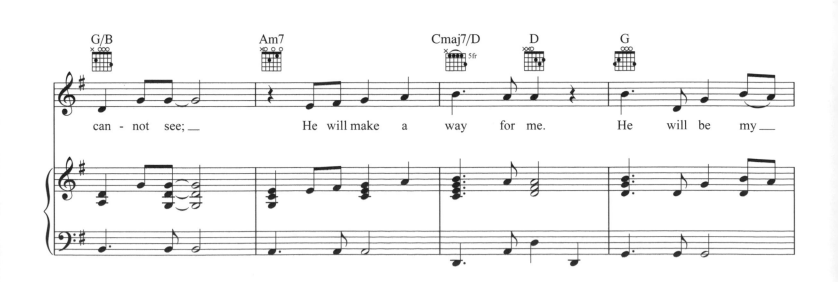

HE IS EXALTED

Words and Music by
TWILA PARIS

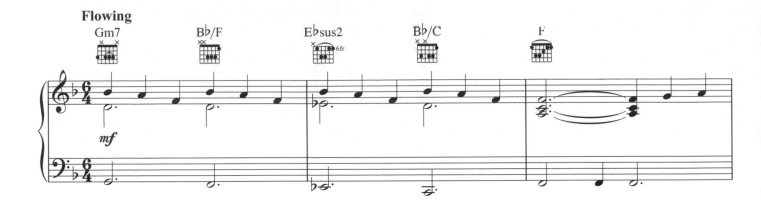

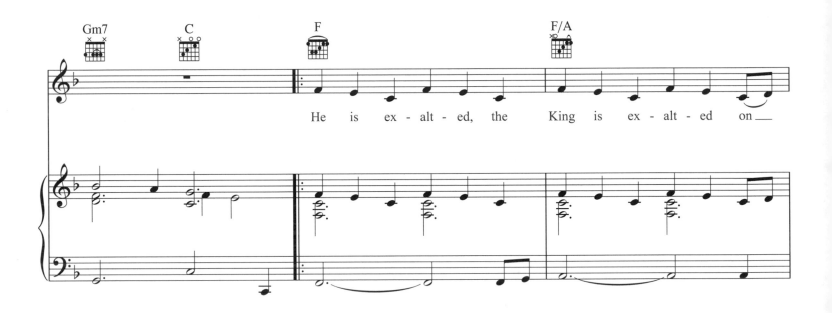

He is ex-alt-ed, the King is ex-alt-ed on __

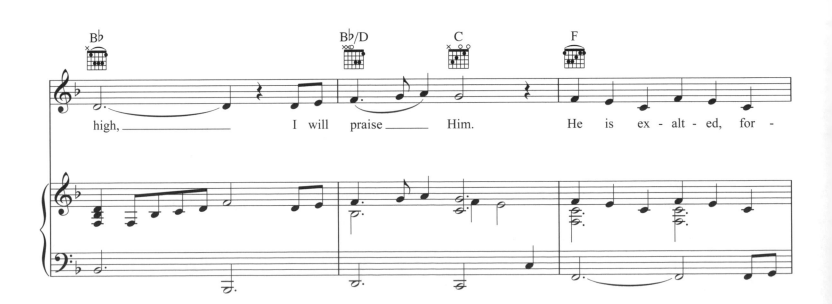

high, _____ I will praise _____ Him. He is ex-alt-ed, for-

I CAN ONLY IMAGINE

Words and Music by
BART MILLARD

HIS STRENGTH IS PERFECT

Words and Music by STEVEN CURTIS CHAPMAN
and JERRY SALLEY

HOW GREAT IS OUR GOD

Words and Music by CHRIS TOMLIN,
JESSE REEVES and ED CASH

HOW MAJESTIC IS YOUR NAME

Words and Music by
MICHAEL W. SMITH

Lord, _ our Lord, _ how ma - jes - tic is Your name _ in all _____ the ___

God,   O _____ Lord _____ God   Al - might -

y. _____

IN CHRIST ALONE

Words and Music by KEITH GETTY
and STUART TOWNEND

LAMB OF GOD

Words and Music by
TWILA PARIS

ON MY KNEES

Words and Music by NICOLE C. MULLEN,
DAVID MULLEN and MICHAEL OCHS

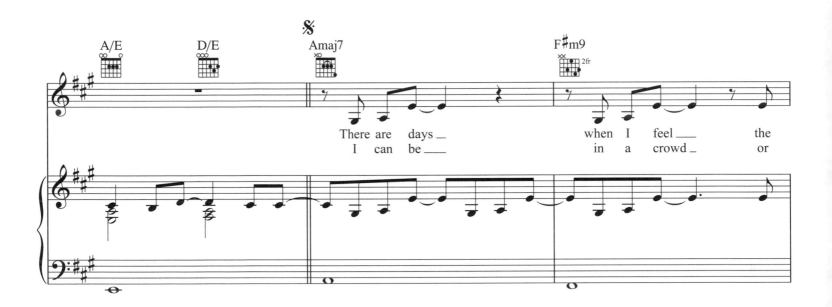

There are days ___ when I feel ___ the
I can be ___ in a crowd ___ or

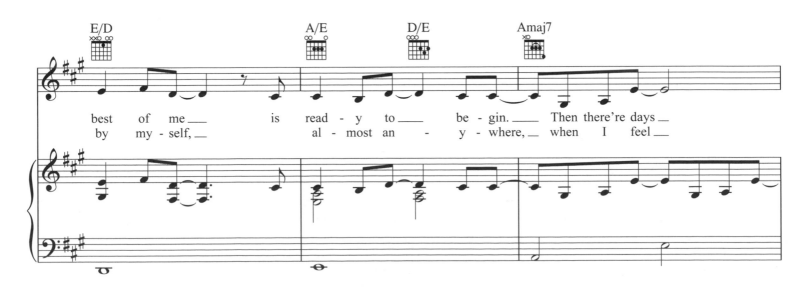

best of me ___ is read-y to ___ be - gin. ___ Then there're days ___
by my-self, ___ al - most an - y - where, when I feel ___

PEOPLE NEED THE LORD

Words and Music by PHILL McHUGH
and GREG NELSON

10,000 REASONS
(Bless the Lord)

Words and Music by JONAS MYRIN
and MATT REDMAN

Moderate Ballad

Bless the Lord, O my soul, O _____ my soul.

Wor-ship His ho-ly name. ___ Sing like nev-er be-fore,

O my soul. I'll wor-ship Your ho-ly name. ___

MY SAVIOR MY GOD

Words and Music by
AARON SHUST

THERE IS A REDEEMER

Words and Music by
MELODY GREEN

There is a re-deem - er,
Je - sus, my re-deem - er,
When I stand in glo - ry,
There is a re-deem - er,

Je - sus, God's own Son.
Name a - bove all names.
I will see His face.
Je - sus, God's own Son. And

THY WORD

Words and Music by MICHAEL W. SMITH
and AMY GRANT

Please be near me to the end. _____
I will love You to the end. _____

VIA DOLOROSA

Words and Music by BILLY SPRAGUE
and NILES BOROP

THERE'S SOMETHING ABOUT THAT NAME

Words by WILLIAM J. and GLORIA GAITHER
Music by WILLIAM J. GAITHER

1. Je - sus, Je - sus, Je - sus; there's just
2.,3. (See additional lyrics)

some - thing __ a - bout that name. ____

Additional Lyrics (Spoken)

2. Jesus... the mere mention of His name can calm the storm, heal the broken, raise the dead. At the name of Jesus, I've seen sin-hardened men melted, derelicts transformed, the lights of hope put back into the eyes of a hopeless child.

At the name of Jesus, hatred and bitterness turned to love and forgiveness, arguments cease.

I've heard a mother softly breathe His name at the bedside of a child delirious from fever, and I've watched that little body grow quiet and the fevered brow cool.

I've sat beside a dying saint, her body racked with pain, who in those final fleeting seconds summoned her last ounce of ebbing strength to whisper earth's sweetest name: Jesus, Jesus...

3. Emperors have tried to destroy it, philosophies have tried to stamp it out. Tyrants have tried to wash it from the face of the earth with the very blood of those who claimed it. Yet still it stands.

And there shall be that final day when every voice that has ever uttered a sound—every voice of Adam's race—shall raise in one great mighty chorus to proclaim the name of Jesus, for in that day "Every knee shall bow and every tongue shall confess that Jesus Christ is Lord!"

So you see, it was not mere chance that caused the angel one night long ago to say to a virgin maiden, "His name shall be called Jesus." Jesus, Jesus, Jesus. You know, there is something about that name.